IMAGES
of America

# HIGH PLAINS
# ARBORETUM

Taryn Lackey and Zander Cline walk through the towering cottonwoods at the entrance of the High Plains Arboretum as they take their engagement photographs in the fall of 2021. Located west of Cheyenne, Wyoming, at 8301 Hildreth Road, these historic trees stand as a living legacy to the horticultural research conducted at the Cheyenne Horticultural Field Station from 1930 to 1974. (Courtesy of Janelle Rose Photography.)

ON THE COVER: This photograph of Robert Minnick in the vegetable plots was featured on the cover of a 1942 publication titled *Vegetable Culture and Varieties for Wyoming*. Minnick was a farm laborer at the station for many years. He helped with horticultural tasks and general maintenance. He worked as a night watchman in the fall to make sure the greenhouse heater had adequate coal and to chase off trespassers trying to steal vegetables from the experimental plots. (Courtesy of US Department of Agriculture, Agricultural Research Service.)

# IMAGES of America
# HIGH PLAINS ARBORETUM

Jessica Friis and the
Friends of the Cheyenne Botanic Gardens

Copyright © 2021 by Jessica Friis and the Friends of the Cheyenne Botanic Gardens
ISBN 978-1-5402-5233-3

Published by Arcadia Publishing
Charleston, South Carolina

Library of Congress Control Number: 2022931443

For all general information, please contact Arcadia Publishing:
Telephone 843-853-2070
Fax 843-853-0044
E-mail sales@arcadiapublishing.com
For customer service and orders:
Toll-Free 1-888-313-2665

Visit us on the Internet at www.arcadiapublishing.com

*To Larry Griffith and Scott Skogerboe, who have worked for decades to preserve and propagate the trees and shrubs growing in the arboretum.*

# Contents

| | | |
|---|---|---|
| Acknowledgments | | 6 |
| Introduction | | 7 |
| 1. | Building an Oasis on the Plains | 9 |
| 2. | People at the Station | 29 |
| 3. | Ditches and Sprinklers, Irrigation at the Station | 51 |
| 4. | Civilian Conservation Corps | 63 |
| 5. | Weather on the High Plains | 73 |
| 6. | Battling the Wind with Shelterbelts and Grasses | 79 |
| 7. | Growing Year-Round in the Greenhouse | 95 |
| 8. | Vegetables, Flowers, and Small Fruits | 103 |
| 9. | The Arboretum, a Living Legacy | 117 |
| Bibliography | | 127 |

# Acknowledgments

The images in this volume, unless otherwise noted, are courtesy of the US Department of Agriculture, Agricultural Research Service. I would like to thank Justin Derner, Pam Freeman, and Shane Hott of the High Plains Grasslands Research Station for giving me access to their collection of historical photographs and records. Much of the information in the captions came from the station log, Civilian Conservation Corps (CCC) reports, and numerical index of station photographs, helping me piece together the stories behind the pictures. Special acknowledgment goes to Larry Griffith and Scott Skogerboe, who have spent more hours among the plants in the arboretum than anyone else alive and were willing to help with this project. I am grateful for Jill Lovato's and Susan Hammel's proofreading assistance. Thank you to Bill Powers, Jennifer Bradford, and Mark Merric for providing photographs of their family. I appreciate Shane Smith, Dick Hart, and Jerry Schuman for sharing their stories with me. Brad Brooks, Clint Bassett, and Erin Lamb of the Cheyenne Board of Public Utilities were happy to educate me on the history of Cheyenne's water supply and give me a tour of the Roundtop facilities. Kim Storey at the Laramie County Library was a great help in finding old articles for my research. Thanks to Janelle Rose for taking photographs of the arboretum. Lastly, a big thank-you to Tina Worthman, who came up with the idea for this book and gave me the time and resources to make it a reality.

# Introduction

For decades after the Homestead Act, many settlers had tried and failed to establish roots in the arid plains of Nebraska, Kansas, Colorado, South Dakota, and Wyoming. The combination of short growing seasons, unpredictable early and late frosts, low precipitation, high winds, and lack of winter snow cover made it especially hard for trees to survive, even those that were hardy enough to survive higher altitudes in the neighboring Rocky Mountains and colder regions of the eastern United States. After several growing seasons of failed attempts to establish plantings, many settlers gave up and left the area. Hoping to help settlers feel at home and beautify budding communities, experimental stations were started in several locations from Canada down to Oklahoma. Their purpose was to find or develop plants that could survive the harsh conditions of the high plains.

The idea for a horticultural research station in Cheyenne came from attorney George E. Brimmer, a man passionate about community beautification. His close friend and business associate, Wyoming senator Francis E. Warren, was a master of the political technique known as "pork barreling," a term used to describe the use of general taxpayer funds for the benefit of a particular area. Warren was able to use his influence as chair of the Senate Appropriations Committee during the 1920s to secure support for a horticultural station near Cheyenne. Since a dryland agricultural research station already existed at Archer, about 10 miles east of Cheyenne, the new station was to focus solely on horticulture. On March 19, 1928, the bill was signed, which authorized $100,000 for the US Department of Agriculture (USDA) to establish an experimental station near Cheyenne, Wyoming. The mission was to experiment with and propagate shade, ornamental, fruit and shelterbelt trees, shrubs, vines, and vegetables adapted to the semiarid regions of the United States. The City of Cheyenne leased 2,139 acres of land to the USDA for 199 years. Wastewater from the Roundtop filtration plant would be available for irrigation at no cost. The station was named the Central Great Plains Field Station to complement the Northern Great Plains Field Station in Mandan, North Dakota, and the Southern Great Plains Field Station at Woodward, Oklahoma. Construction began in 1928 under the direction of Supt. Robert Wilson, an arboriculturist who came from the experimental station at Mandan, North Dakota. Wilson brought seedlings from Mandan to plant the first shelterbelt at the station.

In 1930, the station name was changed to Cheyenne Horticultural Field Station, and Aubrey Clare Hildreth became the superintendent. The first plantings of fruits and vegetables began in 1930. He began extensive breeding programs to develop varieties of fruits, vegetables, and ornamental plants that could thrive in Cheyenne's challenging climate. Station staff tested native plants and cultured varieties from around the region as well as foreign plants collected from similar climates around the world and introduced by USDA plant explorers. In 1936, the role of the station was broadened to include forage crop research, and over 200 varieties of grasses were evaluated for yield potential, cold and drought tolerance, and nutritive value.

The CCC had two camps at the station during the Great Depression. Camp NA2W was a veterans camp and assisted with the daily labor needs at the station from the summer of 1935 until July 1942. Camp SP4 was a junior CCC camp that worked primarily on Roundtop State Park from August 1935 until September 1937. The Army organized and managed the camps, and the USDA planned the work to be done.

In 1942, Hildreth and five members of the staff were assigned to Salinas, California, to study the guayule plant as a possible rubber source during World War II, hoping to reduce US dependence on foreign rubber supplies. During this time, Myron F. Babb served as acting superintendent. Upon his return, Hildreth continued to develop the horticultural research program at the station and wrote the weekly Hildreth Column in the *Wyoming Eagle* newspaper.

From 1955 to 1957, the USDA sent Hildreth to work with the director of agriculture in Kabul, Afghanistan, to help start agricultural experiment stations and research programs in a similarly harsh climate. During his absence, Gerald B. Brown served as acting superintendent. After returning from Afghanistan, Hildreth retired in 1959 to become director of the Denver Botanic Gardens, and Lawrence A. Schaal was named superintendent in 1960. In 1962, the results of 28 years of fruit tree testing were published.

In 1964, Gene Howard became the superintendent of the station, and under his direction, many varieties of plants were released that had been tested and developed over the previous three decades. In 1974, the focus of the station was changed to livestock grazing management, water conservation, and mine land reclamation research. The horticulture and shelterbelt research programs were terminated. With these changes came a new name, the High Plains Grasslands Research Station. Rangeland research continues at the station under the Agricultural Research Service, US Department of Agriculture.

When the focus of the station shifted away from horticulture, most of the horticultural plots were re-seeded to native grasses. After sending cuttings to other stations in the region, all but a few of the fruit trees in the orchards were bulldozed. The trees and shrubs in the arboretum were left standing, and members of the staff continued to till the arboretum and irrigate during dry spells. Despite these efforts, almost half of the trees and shrubs inventoried in 1974 had died by the turn of the century.

In 2000, a group of concerned citizens formed in an attempt to save the trees remaining in the arboretum portion of the station and preserve the historic nature of the space. Calling themselves the Friends of the High Plains Arboretum, they operated as a committee of the Friends of the Cheyenne Botanic Gardens, a nonprofit foundation. Grant funding was used to hire Herb Schaal, a nationally known landscape architect, to draw up a master plan in 2003. After several years of negotiations between Shane Smith, director of the Cheyenne Botanic Gardens (CBG); Lynn Simons, chair of the Friends of the CBG board; Jerry Schuman, location leader of the High Plains Grasslands Research Station; and Will Blackburn, area director of the Northern Great Plains Agricultural Research Service, the lease was amended to return 62 acres of land encompassing the arboretum to the City of Cheyenne. The space was named the High Plains Arboretum and opened to the public in 2008. Since that time, the Cheyenne Urban Forestry Division and Cheyenne Botanic Gardens have worked together with limited funding to preserve the remaining trees and plants, replace some of those lost, and provide interpretative signage for visitors. In 2016, the greenhouse, lath house, and pump house buildings were also returned to the City of Cheyenne. With future funding, the arboretum can be made more accessible with paths, parking lots, and restrooms. The hope is that the greenhouse and lath house buildings can also be restored and used again. All profits and royalties from this book will go to the maintenance of the High Plains Arboretum. To donate to the High Plains Arboretum, please contact the Friends of the Cheyenne Botanic Gardens.

# One
# BUILDING AN OASIS ON THE PLAINS

The sign at the east entrance of the station is pictured on August 1, 1940, after CCC Camp SP4 had built and landscaped the portal. The station was part of a nationwide system of agricultural experiment stations under the direction of land-grant universities, forestry divisions, and eventually, the US Department of Agriculture, as authorized by the Hatch Act of 1887.

The buildings at the station were designed by preeminent Cheyenne architect William R. Dubois, who also designed over 200 other notable structures and residences in Cheyenne and throughout Wyoming. Many are now listed in the National Register of Historic Places. His most recognizable buildings include the Atlas Theater, Cheyenne High School, the City and County Building and Federal Office Building in Cheyenne, and the Wyoming State Insane Asylum (renamed the Wyoming State Hospital) in Evanston. (Courtesy of J.E. Stimson Collection, Wyoming State Archives.)

On October 27, 1928, men are filling the sewer line with a drag plow. The team of horses on the opposite side of the trench, behind the tractor, help hold the drag in place. Throughout the 1940s, work on the station was completed with a combination of horsepower and tractors. The temporary office building is on the right, and haystacks are visible in the fields in the background.

In August 1928, framing for the office (center) is underway, with the exterior of the foreman's house (left) almost complete and the temporary office visible on the right. Most of the scientific staff had offices in this building, and a large conference room is on the first floor. The building is still used for these purposes today.

In the fall of 1928, the porch of the superintendent's house (right) is being constructed. The trench for the sewer line is on the left. Poles for the telephone and electric lines stand in the background.

On May 17, 1929, men excavate for the storage cellar. Although tractors and heavy machinery were used for some of the construction, much of the work was still done by hand. Hundreds of young trees for the shelterbelt program were dug up from the nursery in the fall and stored in the cellar until they were distributed to cooperative sites the following spring. In addition to root crops like potatoes and onions, witloof chicory and rhubarb were also stored in the cellar over the winter.

On May 24, 1929, reinforcing steel is being placed for the walls of the storage cellar. Eight-inch ventilator pipes are visible in the walls next to where the men are working.

Many hands are needed to place the forms for the storage cellar walls on May 24, 1929. The rear of the mess hall (left) and the bunkhouse (right) are visible in the background, with a pole for the power lines between the two buildings. These buildings originally housed and fed station staff, but the mess hall is now used for USDA staff offices, and the bunkhouse became the lab building.

Men pour the concrete slab for the roof of the storage cellar on June 12, 1929. The central ventilating box is on the right. The finished barn is in the background.

On June 13, 1929, the cow barn addition and west end of the stable are shown from the west. Horses used for work on the station were housed here, and cows were kept to provide milk and meat for the mess hall.

On October 4, 1928, the implement shed and seed house unit had been constructed and is shown here from the northeast. This building also had space for a shop. The sewer trench in the right foreground crosses the waterline, which is outlined by the ridge of earth extending from the shed door on the left.

On October 7, 1930, gravel is loaded into dump wagons over a trap in the gravel pit. The top of one wagon is just visible at left. A second wagon is directly under the trap in the center, where the three men are standing.

The gravel just loaded at the pit is dumped on the road toward the east entrance. The field has been plowed in preparation for planting.

Pictured on September 28, 1940, the shop, seed house, and implement shed form a U-shaped building, which is viewed from the southeast. This building is still used by the USDA for equipment storage and maintenance.

The root cellar and storage cellar are pictured in 1939. The original cellar (left), completed in 1929, had been recently expanded (right) by CCC Camp NA2W.

The bunkhouse (above) and mess hall (below) are pictured on September 28, 1940. Many staff members resided in these buildings. Board was $5 a month and was deducted from their paychecks. Visitors to the station from other government divisions could also stay overnight. The station log mentioned a mess club, which had officers. On January 18, 1938, Benedict got a new Ping Pong outfit, and residents of the bunkhouse resumed their slam-bang brand of the game, which was interrupted some months previous when all the equipment was broken. On the morning of Sunday, January 16, 1938, it was reported that all clients of the mess failed to show up for breakfast (presumably because they slept in), which left the cook, Sadie Witte, very unhappy. Sadie's husband, Herman, also worked at the station as a farm laborer. Mess club prices were 25¢ for meals and 5¢ for milk.

On September 28, 1940, the farm foreman's cottage, occupied at that time by principal scientific aide John D. Kelso and his wife, is fully landscaped. Kelso was the station handyman and often built new equipment out of scraps to meet the needs of staff. The station log mentions several stag parties for station employees happening at the Kelso residence.

The office building (left) and clerk's cottage (right) are pictured on August 16, 1933. The clerk's cottage was occupied by the pathologist, Dr. Guy W. Bohn, and his wife. Dr. Bohn stayed in the bunkhouse when he first arrived at the station until his wife was able to join him, at which point they moved into this house. The station log mentions him passing out cigars to celebrate the birth of a baby boy on September 13, 1939.

Pictured in August 1940, the superintendent's residence was occupied by Dr. Hildreth and his family. This was the largest house on the station, and the superintendent often entertained guests at the residence. Gene Howard also lived in this house while he was superintendent of the station.

This view of the station lawn was taken from the north-facing windows in the office in September 1933. The superintendent's house (center) and staff house one (right) are in the background. Dr. James E. Kraus, an assistant physiologist, lived in staff house one with his wife and children. The numbering for the staff houses was switched at some point, and this became staff house three. This house was home to Dick and Helen Hart, with their two children, for 18 years.

On December 1, 1928, the office (left), staff house one (center), and staff house two (right) were being constructed. Dr. Myron F. Babb, associate physiologist, and his wife, Georgiana, lived in staff house two. She often traveled with him on business trips. Their engagement and marriage were mentioned in the station log in May 1936. On May 28, a stag party for Myron was held at Kelso's house and attended by station employees.

Staff house three (now called staff house one), pictured on August 1, 1940, was occupied by geneticist LeRoy Powers and his family. His two children, William "Bill" and Margaret "Peggy," were raised here. Bill remembers being able to roam the station freely as a child, playing with the children of other staff and visiting his father in the office building when he wanted to speak with him during the day.

A pathological laboratory was built in the basement of the bunkhouse when Guy Bohn began working at the station in 1938. It is pictured here on September 30, 1940, with the inoculation room on the right. The lab was used by station staff until 2006.

This view of the opposite side of the pathological laboratory shows the microscope table (left), doorway to the incubation room (center), and storage cabinets (right). The microscope cost $1,016 when it was purchased in 1938.

The interior of the incubation and germination room is pictured on September 30, 1940. The instrument inside the open chamber recorded temperature and humidity.

Photography equipment at the station included this shadowless background lightbox with support for a five-by-seven-inch view camera suspended overhead. The camera points straight down when on the support. This apparatus was used to take detailed photographs of the fruit, flowers, and leaves of plants grown in station experiments.

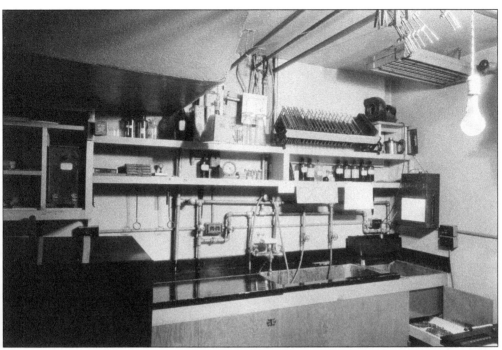

The interior of the darkroom above shows a washing sink and covered water baths for developing trays and tanks, with the heating unit visible in the lower right corner. The view below shows the sink (left); the enlarger (center); and the workbench with Roto print dryer, photomicrographic camera, and arc lamp (right). The long-awaited enlarger was received on October 27, 1937, with much enthusiasm. Vic Hastings, who took many of the station photographs, was on leave when it arrived, so Harris Benedict took joy in assembling it. Benedict wanted to enlarge photographs taken with a Leica camera on his European tour the previous summer. The next day, Hastings was still on leave but could not withstand the charm and allure of the new enlarger and came out to tinker with it. His brother, who was visiting from Canada, came with him.

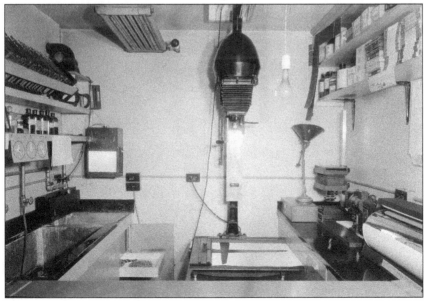

On March 25, 1936, station employees are moving a Bolleana poplar from the side of the office to the rear of the building. They are finishing the job begun a couple of weeks prior by the NA2W CCC crew. The station log lists Swede, Adams, Shomaker, Hagen, Blunt, and Washburn as the men working on the project.

On January 27, 1939, men from CCC Camp NA2W remove a tree to transplant elsewhere on the station. This process required several days of labor for each tree, and the CCC men ended up planting and transplanting hundreds of trees on the station grounds. The license plate on the tractor reads, "U.S.C.C.C."

On June 6, 1932, an unidentified man uses a power lawn mower to maintain the station lawns near the office building. In later years, the station log mentions that Mike Byrne mowed the lawns around station buildings.

On August 3, 1933, two men operate a lawn-sidewalk edger built by station handyman John D. Kelso. He used four pieces of pipe and a cultivator disk to build the machine. A wooden roller on the sidewalk side extended the disc about two inches onto the lawn and threw the turf trimmings onto the sidewalk behind the disk.

On September 14, 1933, this view of flower beds and ornamental plantings on the grounds was taken from the office looking south. These plantings served the dual purpose of beautifying station grounds and developing ornamental plants to make prairie homesteads more livable. The headhouse and greenhouses (left) and mess hall (right) are visible in the background.

The toy wagon on the left of this photograph is evidence of the children who lived and played on the station grounds. This view was taken from the superintendent's residence looking southeast in 1936. The buildings are, from left to right, the office, the foreman's house, the clerk's house, and the superintendent's house.

Taken before construction was completed in November 1929, this view of the station includes, from left to right, the implement shed, the bunkhouse, the mess hall, the barn, the office, the clerk's house, the superintendent's house, and staff houses one and two.

Just four years later, the view of the station on August 16, 1933, showed a remarkable transformation. Shelterbelts, landscaping, and trial blocks had been planted. The buildings, now complete, are, from left to right following the curve of the drive, the implement shed, the bunkhouse, the mess hall, a garage behind them, the barn, the roof of the storage cellar, the office, the clerk's house and garage, the superintendent's house, and staff houses one, two, and three, with garages behind them.

By 1939, the plantings had grown substantially. In this photograph, the headhouse, with a tall chimney, and greenhouses are visible on the left, and the lath house is the white building to the right of the headhouse.

By 1960, the trees at the station had grown to the point that the buildings were no longer visible. Many of these trees still stand, and the station has become its own unique microclimate on the prairie. Protected from the wind by a man-made forest, a herd of mule deer and many birds have made it their home for decades.

# Two
# People at the Station

Pres. Franklin D. Roosevelt visited Cheyenne on Sunday, October 11, 1936. He is shaking hands with Rev. C.A. Bennett (left) of the Episcopal Church where he attended services with his daughter-in-law Betsey (center), and his wife, Eleanor (right). After the services, they toured Fort Warren, the horticultural station, and the CCC camp. The president greeted Dr. Hildreth, the staff, and their wives at the office. He then gave a speech at Fort Warren to a crowd of 20,000 people. The population of Cheyenne at the time was 16,000. (Courtesy of Brammar Collection, Wyoming State Archives.)

Aubrey C. Hildreth became superintendent of the station in 1930. His prior research in hardiness and cold resistance of apple varieties, dry-land plant production, and improving native species of blueberries made him a perfect fit for the research program at Cheyenne. Hildreth encouraged his staff to pursue graduate studies and participate in national and international conferences. His ability to gently instruct in a casual manner laced with wit and dry humor was appreciated by his employees, who often referred to him as "Doc." He traveled frequently, visiting cooperative sites, collaborating with other agencies and researchers, and giving talks to anyone who requested it, from Girl Scouts and small garden clubs to international horticultural societies. When present at the station, he helped collect data and plan future research. He gave visitors tours of the station and answered questions from the public. Upon retirement from the USDA in 1959, he became the director of the Denver Botanic Gardens in its infancy. He passed away in 1975 at the age of 81, having received multiple national awards for his contributions to horticulture.

Gene Howard came to Cheyenne in 1937 with $9 in his pocket and the clothes on his back. He began working at what is now known as the Frontier Refinery. In 1950, he joined the team of technicians at the Cheyenne Horticultural Field Station and started a new career. After working under Hildreth, he became the superintendent in 1964. Under his direction, many varieties of plants were introduced to the public, a culmination of decades of research at the station. Those introductions included mums, lilacs, strawberries, raspberries, phlox, geraniums, and carnations. In 1974, Gene Howard supervised the transition in focus from horticulture to range management. Jerry Shuman remembers that Howard had a distinct Oklahoma accent and was quite a hunter. Even on hunting trips Howard was always looking for new plants. He took cuttings or seed from every interesting plant he saw.

Sen. Gale McGee and his wife, Loraine, are pictured during a visit to the station in the summer of 1963. Senator McGee represented Wyoming in the US Senate from 1959 to 1977. When the USDA attempted to close the horticultural station in 1965 and 1969, McGee fought hard to keep it open. Using his influence as a member of the Senate Appropriations Committee and the Agriculture Appropriations Subcommittee, he was able to find funds to keep the station in operation.

Joseph O'Mahoney, pictured in 1937, was a Democratic US senator from Wyoming. When plans were announced that the veterans CCC camp located at the station would be moved to Green River, O'Mahoney worked to keep the camp in Cheyenne. He also accompanied President Roosevelt during his visit to Cheyenne in 1936. (Courtesy of Wyoming State Archives.)

Dr. Myron F. Babb, a vegetable specialist, stands at the workbench in the new root cellar on January 20, 1942. Babb was one of the earliest researchers at the station, having started in 1930. He remained at the station until 1948 and was the acting superintendent during Hildreth's temporary assignment to California from 1942 to 1945. He conducted many studies on vegetables over the years, testing different varieties, growing methods, and effects of fertilization.

Dr. LeRoy Powers (right) examines snapdragons in the greenhouse with an unidentified young man. Powers often hired high school and college students or CCC enrollees temporarily to help collect and organize data from his experiments. Some of the young men who started in this capacity ended up getting permanent positions later on. John Callaghan started as a calculator before he graduated high school, and Dick Taylor started in 1938 typing manuscripts. They were both regular employees by 1940. (Courtesy of the Powers family.)

Dr. LeRoy Powers stands with his wife, Rena, daughter Margaret "Peggy," and son William "Bill" outside their home on the station in 1939. He was a respected statistician and plant geneticist who bred fruits and vegetables from 1934 to 1953. During the war, he and his family went to California with Hildreth to research the guayule plant as a possible rubber source. He left Cheyenne for the USDA sugar beet research unit on the campus of Colorado State University and was instrumental in expanding that program. (Courtesy of the Powers family.)

Bill and Peggy Powers are pictured at Roundtop Reservoir. They moved to the station when Peggy was three, and the station log mentions Dr. Powers passing around cigars when Bill was born in 1936. They left for Colorado during Bill's senior year. Bill earned a doctorate and spent his career studying and teaching the relationships between water and soil at Kansas State University and the University of Nebraska. His work is featured in *Advanced Soil Physics* by Ron Kirkham, published in 1972. (Courtesy of the Powers family.)

Richard and James Hildreth play on the lawn between the staff houses on August 1, 1940. These boys lost their mother during their time here. Marie Hildreth passed away on June 9, 1936, after giving birth by Cesarean section to James. Her body was brought to the living room of the residence before the funeral. The services, conducted by Rev. H.M. Pingree, were held at Worland Mortuary, and she was laid to rest in Lakeview Cemetery. Station staff LeRoy Powers, Harris Benedict, John Kelso, Vic Hastings, Jim Kraus, and W.D. Roney were pallbearers. The many floral tributes were beautiful, and the chapel was filled to capacity by station employees and friends of the family. Richard and James had two older brothers, John and Robert, who were young when the family arrived at the station in 1930. Dr. Hildreth remarried in 1944 to Isabel Rickard and had a daughter, Judith, both of whom accompanied him to Afghanistan.

Frank W. Carruth, an assistant clerk, managed the CCC accounts for Camp NA2W. He married in 1936 while employed at the station. In the station log on February 25, 1938, the sewer in the basement of the house occupied by Carruth backfired in his face while he attempted to flush it out during the noon hour. No major damage was done, although Carruth described as "considerable" the amount of the sewer's contents that landed in his right eye. Boric acid baths during the afternoon somewhat alleviated this discomfort, he reported.

Agent J.V. "Vic" Hastings is pictured in his office on September 30, 1940. Plant accession records and catalog files are in the background. In addition to his work with ornamentals and fruit trees, he was the station photographer. Many of the photographs in this book were taken by him. The Marchant calculator in the front left of the photograph was mentioned in the log and purchased new for over $500 at a time when some station employees were only paid $100 a month.

Dr. James "Jim" E. Kraus, assistant physiologist, sits at his desk on September 30, 1940, with a bank of seed storage cabinets on the left wall. On March 31, 1938, a shower was held for Jim's wife, Marian, to celebrate their recent adoption of a baby. He worked with Powers and Babb on vegetable studies at the station and cooperative sites around the region. He spent several months at Cornell University earning his doctorate. Marian often accompanied him when he traveled.

Dr. Harris M. Benedict, an associate physiologist in the Division of Forage Crops, worked at the station from 1938 to 1946. Research in forage crops and grasses to prevent soil erosion was popular at the time. Visitors from as far away as China, Australia, and South Africa came to visit the grass plots and learn about his studies. Benedict spent several weeks in Europe in the summer of 1937, visiting grass breeding sites and attending the International Grass Congress.

Andrew "Andy" W. Krofcheck, agent of forestry and shelterbelt research, worked for the station temporarily in 1936 before permanent employment in 1937. Before that, he worked at the Forest Service Nursery in Halsey, Nebraska, and was the superintendent of CCC Camp F37W at Esterbrook, Wyoming, on the north side of Laramie Peak. He traveled frequently to visit shelterbelt cooperators and collect seeds for the shelterbelt nursery. His salary was $155 a month, less $5 a month for living quarters in the bunkhouse.

Wayne M. Guernsey, a senior clerk, sits in the administration office on September 30, 1940. He started at the station on May 4, 1940. In April 1943, he was inducted into the Army. He returned to work at the station after the war. The war effort greatly affected the staff at the station, with the Army also taking Dewey and Krofcheck. Benedict, Powers, Federer, Taylor, and Krouch went to California with Hildreth for the guayule studies.

Gerald "Jerry" B. Brown stands in front of the fume hood in his laboratory in the basement of the office building. He worked for Western Sugar Company in Denver when Hildreth asked to temporarily engage one of their chemists to measure the sugar content of pumpkins. After temporary appointments where he earned $130 per month and stayed in the bunkhouse, he returned home to Longmont to marry before starting a permanent position in December 1937. He worked at the station until 1960 and was acting superintendent while Hildreth was in Afghanistan.

Dr. Guy Weston Bohn, a plant pathologist and geneticist, worked at the station from 1938 to 1946. He participated in vegetable studies at the station and at a cooperative site in Torrington, Wyoming. This pathology lab was installed in the basement of the bunkhouse for him, pictured on September 30, 1940.

Pictured on September 13, 1940, the station regular employees are, from left to right, (first row) unskilled laborer Charles "Chuck" Conine, agent Charles Davis, and farm laborer John Callaghan; (second row) agent Richard "Dick" Taylor; (third row) agent Charles Adams, and farm laborer Robert Minnick; (fourth row) agent Donald "Don" Lauridson and agent Forest Spickelmeier; (fifth row) farm laborer Herman Witte, agent Roland Blake, and agent Arthur Thompson. Many of these men were offered assignments on a seasonal basis until more work was available.

The station temporary employees are, from left to right, (first row) Joseph "Joe" Nichols, Marvin "Levi" Brenner, and Byron "Barney" Hawkins; (second row) Ed Blunt, Carl "Swede" Adolphson, and Michael "Mike" Byrne; (third row) Curtis "Bud" Vaughan and John "Jonnie" Byrne. All were farm laborers, and Swede Adolphson was the farm laborer foreman. Adolphson was mentioned frequently in the station log for getting injured on the job, usually minor cuts and bruises from the nature of tools they used daily.

On September 28, 1940, agents Eldon Krouch (left) and Charles Davis (right) stand in front of the doorway to the headhouse. These two men were the main caretakers of the greenhouses, which are attached to the rear of this building. Davis worked primarily in the greenhouse and on ornamental plantings on the grounds. He made sure the greenhouse stayed heated in the winter. He also helped Kelso with various repairs of furnaces and equipment.

Levi Brenner is driving the wagon with Robert Minnick behind the wagon wheel. The barn is behind them, with a cowshed and corral on the right. Minnick is pictured in the cover photograph of this book. Brenner worked with the horses and livestock and spent many hours in the winter spreading manure on the plots with a team of horses. When weather prohibited outdoor work, he cleaned harnesses and maintained equipment, often assisted by Herman Witte.

Agent Eldon "Don" Krouch examines squash in the greenhouse on September 28, 1940. He started in 1937 as a temporary calculator for Dr. Powers, with an initial salary of $100 per month. He later became a permanent employee and worked primarily in the greenhouse, helping with the breeding experiments. The greenhouse required a lot of work. In addition to watering and pest control year-round, keeping the greenhouses heated in the winter required a person on hand 24 hours a day to feed the boilers with coal. Minnick and Davis were mentioned in the station log as taking the night watch, and Davis was often asking for more coal when the supply started to get low. Two large boilers were in the basement of the headhouse. Individual circulating pumps for each greenhouse forced hot water through pipes running around the greenhouse walls and ceilings. The boilers were later converted to heating oil and eventually removed after an infrared heating system was installed in Greenhouses A and B in 1989. Larry Griffith remembers the boilers and pumps requiring frequent maintenance.

John Kelso was the station handyman and an avid fisherman. On May 3, 1936, he was fishing on upper Horse Creek in Albany County and caught a mess of fair-sized trout. Just after leaving the creek, two tires blew out on one side of the car. Having no tire patches or pump and not on a traveled road, he had to hike six miles to Horse Creek quarry for materials. He got back on the road at 8:00 p.m. and was home by 9:15 p.m. He reported finding plenty of wood ticks.

This is a catch of Wyoming trout, courtesy of John Kelso on June 23, 1940. Several of the station staff enjoyed fishing. Roney reported his catch, and that of others, every weekend when he wrote the log from 1935 to 1937. Babb, Kelso, Powers, Bohn, and Howell frequently went on weekend fishing trips together. Sadie Witte once caught a three-pound trout in Roundtop Reservoir.

Donald "Don" H. Dewey was an agent in the vegetables division from 1940 to 1946, after starting as a temporary hire. He traveled with other staff to scientific meetings and helped in the greenhouse. The station log mentions him being appointed a junior olericulturist. Olericulture is the science of growing vegetables. He served in the Army during the war and then returned to the station.

Judging from accounts in the station log, Jerry Brown seemed to be quite a character. On March 21, 1938, he had a new pipe, which he brandished freely. (His doctor ordered him to quit smoking in 1941.) On May 27, 1937, Vic Hastings showed up with a new 37 Model Chevrolet. Don Krouch and Brown hooked up a joke bomb under the hood, but it did not work—the joke was on them.

On August 11, 1937, the Great Plains section of the American Society for Horticultural Science met at the station, hosting visitors from Minnesota, Colorado, North Dakota, and Canada. Powers leans against the pillar to the right of the door. Kraus (second row, left), Hildreth (second row, holding his hat in his hands), and Krofcheck (third row, left) are seated on the steps. Two cases of Walters beer were served in the field after lunch at Dr. Hildreth's expense. The chamber of commerce provided a complimentary dinner at the Plains Hotel.

On March 16, 1938, a permit was received to import cherry, plum, and crab apple seedlings and scions from Dr. Seager Wheeler in Rosthern, Saskatchewan, Canada. Dr. Wheeler was a famous agronomist known for developing wheat and fruit strains for a short growing season and harsh winters. Having immigrated to Canada from England, his homestead near Rosthern is now a National Historic Site. He developed dryland farming techniques and invented equipment that helped create a sustainable agricultural economy in Saskatchewan.

Gene Howard (left) and Gene Vanderslice (right) are in the greenhouse with carnations in 1976. Research on carnations for the commercial flower industry in Denver started with Hildreth, Brown, and Hastings in the 1930s. Vanderslice also worked with Howard on other horticultural research. Dick Hart and Jerry Schuman both describe Vanderslice as a quiet fellow with a different sense of humor. He transferred to Cheyenne in 1964 after 25 years at the Southern Great Plains Field Station in Woodward, Oklahoma.

Marilyn J. Samuel holds a bough full of fruits from the Dauphin crab apple. She was an incredibly knowledgeable botanist at the station from 1966 to 1988. Richard "Dick" Hart jokes that after too long of a coffee break, he would forget the names of every plant Samuel had taught him. During a course they took together, though, Hart was the only one who could identify an immature ear of corn in formaldehyde, which was the only plant in the quiz that she did not recognize. He will never forget that moment of triumph.

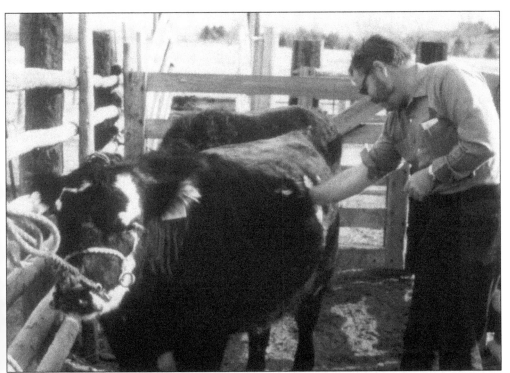

Dick Hart works with Donut (above), a rumen fistulated cow popular among visitors, in 1976. The surgically placed window allowed access to her digestive system. Hart came to the station in 1974, excited to return to research with cattle, after studying the effects of increased ultraviolet radiation on plants. He found that most plants tolerated increased UV, especially wheat and peanuts, so he jokes that if UV radiation gets out of control, people can live off peanut butter sandwiches. Hart became superintendent after Gene Howard retired in 1976 and research had changed to rangeland management. He and Samuel (below) celebrate the opening of the east unit in 1980. Hart was able to secure surplus land from F.E. Warren Air Force Base, a perfect location for studies on rotational grazing practices. Dr. Justin Derner continues this research today.

Field days were a regular event at the station and popular with the public. Trucks loaded with visitors are heading out for an inspection trip of the station on August 8, 1934.

This photograph of the entire group attending the Laramie County Farmers Field Day Party was taken on the lawn in front of the bunkhouse. Agricultural groups from Colorado, Wyoming, and Nebraska visited the station to learn about the research conducted there.

The Daughters of the American Revolution are pictured on September 2, 1933, presenting a George Washington Elm to the State of Wyoming. Gov. Leslie A. Miller accepted the gift.

The Kiwanis Club had a luncheon party at the station on September 7, 1933. Participants are pictured in front of the office building.

In the late 1800s, the USDA began sending plant explorers to the far reaches of the globe to find plants that might have value in the United States. Many plants collected in the cold, dry regions of Russia were instrumental in developing hardy varieties that could thrive on the high plains. Prof. Niels Hansen was the first official USDA plant explorer and traveled across Eastern Europe into Asia eight times, looking for cold and drought-tolerant plants and collecting seeds by the thousands. He directed the government experiment station in Brookings, South Dakota, and taught horticulture at the university there. He referred to the Great Plains as "his American Siberia" and reportedly said, "If it can grow in Siberia, it might survive in South Dakota." He grew and crossbred his introductions, amounting to over 400 plant varieties over the course of his career. His goal was to improve the life of the common man on the Great Plains, and his work changed the landscape of this part of the country. Dr. Hansen came to the station to speak at a meeting of the American Society for Horticultural Science in 1937. (Courtesy of South Dakota Hall of Fame.)

# Three
# DITCHES AND SPRINKLERS, IRRIGATION AT THE STATION

On June 11, 1935, men prepare overhead sprinklers for summer use. They are, from left to right, Jonnie Byrne, unidentified, Robert Minnick, unidentified, and Swede Adolphson. The unidentified men may have been CCC enrollees from Camp NA2W, all of whom were involved in the daily labor at the station. These overhead sprinklers irrigated the nursery plants south of the greenhouses and lath house.

Water from Granite and Crystal Reservoirs flows through a pipeline into the valve house (left), where the volume of water flowing into the city can be controlled. The valve house was constructed from 1902 to 1911 and included living quarters so that an employee could be available 24 hours a day until remote control of the valves was possible. This photograph shows erosion of the soil caused when water was released out of the pipeline onto the hillside. One of the projects of CCC Camp SP4 was to regrade the area to prevent further erosion.

This photograph, taken on November 8, 1929, shows the north side of the Roundtop Water Filtration Plant. The plant was constructed from 1911 to 1915 to clean and treat the water supply coming into the city of Cheyenne. When the filters in the plant needed to be cleaned, water was flushed back through the filters. As part of the lease agreement with the City of Cheyenne, 450 acre feet per year of this wastewater was allotted to the station free of charge for irrigation purposes.

This photograph provides a view of the Roundtop Water Filtration Plant before plantings and grading were added by the CCC in 1935. The fence to the right was surrounding the storage tanks, where water was treated with chlorine to kill pathogens. The square projection on the right side of the building was the settling basin where flocculants were added to bind with dissolved solids in the water and make them heavy enough to settle out. Water then flowed through filters inside the building to catch any remaining particles.

These tanks are curved to prevent the water from becoming stagnant as it flows through and to provide sufficient contact time for the water to be disinfected by chlorine. The tanks are now covered with a roof to prevent visits from waterfowl and hold 11 million gallons of water for Cheyenne's water supply. The station buildings and shelterbelts are visible in the rear of the photograph. An irrigation ditch runs behind the shelterbelts and brings water from Roundtop Reservoir to planting blocks on the south end of the station.

Roundtop Reservoir was constructed to store the wastewater for use in irrigating plants at the station. To create the reservoir, a dam was necessary, and the first step was to build the valve box pictured here. In this September 10, 1930, image, workmen are laying outlet pipeline so that water can be let out of the reservoir through this valve box.

The next step in building the reservoir was to dig trenches at the base of the dam to install the key wall. This wall extends underground to provide a foundation for the dam. The outlet pipeline is visible coming out of the valve box and crossing both trenches.

A large mechanical shovel scoops dirt out of a borrow pit and loads it into dump trucks. The earth was used to build an embankment for the dam, and the borrow pits became the bottom of the reservoir.

On October 7, 1930, dump trucks bring the excavated earth to the site of the dam. The valve box at center-right will be surrounded by the dam. Roundtop Reservoir is located north and west of the Roundtop Filtration Plant, which is visible at the left of the photograph.

A dump truck hauls gravel to cover the surface of the dam, and men place larger rocks, known as riprap, on the side of the dam where the water will contact it. The riprap prevents the motion of the water from eroding the dam over time. The dam was built up around the valve box, and the top of the box is visible behind the team of horses on the left.

The opposite side of the dam is visible here. Horses and a tractor pull equipment to grade the dam while a dump truck brings gravel. The outlet gate is below where the horses are working. The purpose of this outlet gate is to let water out if the reservoir becomes too full and risks overflowing the dam.

Once the dam was completed, wastewater from the Roundtop Filtration Plant flows out of the covered 24-inch pipeline into the reservoir supply ditch.

On May 6, 1931, the reservoir is filled with water, and the completed dam is in the background. The top of the valve box is visible in the center of the dam.

On December 5, 1929, workmen stand inside a trench coming from the south outlet of Roundtop Reservoir. Behind them is the valve that lets water from the reservoir out into the concrete irrigation ditches. Water can be directed southwest to irrigate the planting blocks at the far south end of the station, or southeast to water the arboretum.

The Civil Works Administration (CWA) was a New Deal job creation program that provided temporary manual-labor jobs to unemployed workers during the winter of 1933–1934. CWA workers dig and line up the irrigation ditch east of the main inlet box on December 29, 1933.

This general view (above) of CWA workers filling the irrigation ditch with concrete is dated February 3, 1934, and shows the ditch winding through the field on the west side of Roundtop, which is visible in the background. The ditch carries water from Roundtop Reservoir to the station grounds. The truck in the foreground pulls a warm water storage tank for mixing concrete. The concrete mixer sits in the center of the photograph, and the truck in the background hauls manure. Since this work was being done in the middle of winter, the freshly poured concrete ditches and forms were covered with manure to reduce frost damage during the night (below).

A finished irrigation ditch, lined with concrete, is pictured here. The control gate is open (center), and the side outlet (left) is closed. This arrangement allows the water to continue flowing downstream. In order to flood irrigate this field, the control gate would be closed and the side outlet opened to direct the water onto the field. Larry Griffith still uses this flood irrigation system to water the trees in the arboretum.

Irrigation water enters the plots in the fields. These plots were planted with various grasses for studies in the prevention of erosion. Dikes were formed in the soil to direct irrigation water.

CWA workers load up wagons in the gravel pit for roadwork around Roundtop on December 29, 1933 (above), and are pictured working on those roads in January 1934 (below). Although the CWA program only lasted for one winter, thousands of miles of roads, levees, and water pipelines were built all over the country. The program also included projects that built or improved schools and airports. Funding for these projects came from the Public Works Administration, the Federal Emergency Relief Administration, and Congress. After the very impactful and successful program was terminated in the summer of 1934, work carried on under some of the same administrative leadership in the form of the Works Progress Administration in 1935.

East of the greenhouse, a reservoir named Chilcott Lake was built to supply water for the sprinkler systems irrigating the nursery and station lawns. The small building behind the reservoir is the pump house, which pumped water into the sprinkler systems. On July 15, 1932, the reservoir of the pump house is filled with water, with the shelterbelt nursery visible in the background. The pump house still stands, but Chilcott Lake is dry.

The overhead sprinkler system is in operation with an oscillator in the foreground. Water jets, though faint in this photograph, can be seen along the pipe. Part of the pump house reservoir, Chilcott Lake, is visible at left and was filled with water from Roundtop Reservoir.

# Four
# CIVILIAN CONSERVATION CORPS

Two enrollees from CCC Camp SP4 remove trees from nearby mountains for transplanting within Roundtop Park in November 1935. Over the course of 25 days, they removed and transported 350 native evergreen trees to Roundtop. The "SP" in SP4 stood for "state park." The purpose of this camp was to improve the area around Roundtop, creating a state park for the public to enjoy.

There were two CCC camps located at the station, SP4 and NA2W. SP4 was a junior camp, and NA2W was a veterans camp. Junior CCC enrollees were unmarried, unemployed males 18–25 years of age, usually from urban areas of the country. Most of the men in Camp SP4 came from Oklahoma or Ohio. To apply for the veterans camp, men had to be certified by the Veterans Administration and could be any age, married or single, as long as they needed work. Enrollees signed up for a six-month period and could reenroll up to four times if unable to find permanent employment. The CCC camp buildings were located near the east entrance of the station and housed living quarters, a mess hall, a library, and educational space. The station log reports that about 30 men from Camp NA2W went on strike to protest the quality of the camp food in August 1936. The men who protested were dishonorably discharged, but that same week, the station began donating surplus produce from the experimental plots to the camp for meals. Whether or not that was coincidental is unclear.

On January 20, 1942, Dennis, from CCC Camp NA2W, feeds the furnace in a cellar. This was a risky job. The station log recorded multiple incidents of employees smashing toes or fingers when a lump of coal fell from a bin. CCC enrollees unloaded a railroad car full of coal every 10–14 days throughout the winter months to heat station buildings. The "NA" portion of Camp NA2W stood for "national arboretum" under the Bureau of Plant Industry, and this camp provided daily labor at the station from summer 1935 until July 1942. They transplanted hundreds of trees; performed horticultural tasks like weeding, spreading manure, and cleaning seed; helped with regular maintenance of station buildings; constructed and maintained roads and irrigation systems; and built the lath house and addition to the storage cellar. Although little is known about the man pictured, he represents hundreds of unidentified CCC enrollees who performed hours of manual labor in Wyoming's natural elements to make the station beautiful and functional.

Dated September 1935, this image shows Camp SP4 men preparing the soil for tree planting. The tools in this photograph did not arrive at the camp when the men did. Camp superintendent Mosher Edwards wrote in his November 1935 report, "The camp was occupied by Company 3852 from Oklahoma but in August they were seriously handicapped by not having a complete technical force and by an insufficient supply of hand tools. In September these problems were remedied and during the months of October and November the work has gone ahead steadily."

The September 1935 report stated, "We have also been encouraged by numerous, gratifying reports on the conduct of the enrollees. Although we are looking forward anxiously to the development work of the park area, we have not lost sight of the fact that our chief responsibility lies in the development of manhood rather than State Parks. . . . We have an unusually fine group of enrolled men who seem to be not only willing but anxious to cooperate with the supervisory and facilitating personnel in every way possible."

In September 1935, Camp SP4 men remove topsoil for use on Roundtop. Harold Thatcher, educational advisor of the camp, put it this way in the June 1936 report, "Life in the CCC is not designed to be permanent, but it is temporary to the individual in that he is to seek and secure employment at the earliest possible date and make room for some other deserving boy in this 'School in the Woods.' The technical service has cooperated at every opportunity in the interest and welfare of the enrollee."

Camp SP4 enrollees work on bank sloping at Roundtop State Park in August 1935. The loam removed from the banks of the ditch was used as a seedbed for the tree planting areas. The clay was used for fills in the park roads. It was estimated that 4,000 square yards of dirt were moved. CCC enrollees were paid $30 a month, with $25 of that sent home to their families. Food, clothing, housing, medical care, and education were provided by the camp.

CCC Camp SP4 enrollees dig irrigation ditches on Roundtop to soak the land in preparation for tree planting. According to the camp superintendent, the City of Cheyenne and surrounding community showed unusual interest and eagerness to cooperate with the program. The local newspapers covered the camps, and neighboring ranchers willingly gave trees and stone from their ranches for park use. Dr. Hildreth was the state park authority for this camp.

On September 4, 1935, CCC enrollees grade the supply ditch for Roundtop Reservoir. Education of enrollees took place outside of the workday. This camp had a typing class, and each member had to pay 50¢ a month to rent a typewriter. Classes in algebra, shorthand, woodworking, and drafting were also offered.

In January 1936, Camp SP4 prepares a roadbed by hand. Frozen ground and sandstone ledges slowed the progress to such an extent that it was necessary to acquire a road plow and blasting supplies to expedite the work. Despite the laborious nature of the project, Foreman Jack Wallace was able to create enthusiasm and interest in road construction and terracing. Enrollees studied engineering treatises during their leisure time, and Foreman Wallace assisted in classroom discussions.

Two Camp SP4 enrollees plow dirt for soil preparation in March 1936. The purchase of a plow helped considerably in hastening the work. Recreation programs helped increase company morale. Inter-barrack boxing and baseball teams were organized to compete with teams from Fort F.E. Warren and Cheyenne. The baseball team from Camp SP4 frequently beat the team from the station. The Cheyenne ministry furnished a short sermon at camp each Tuesday evening.

Table and bench combinations are under construction (above) in January 1936. The CCC did not have a carpenter shop, so construction was carried on in a tent, which was too small to assemble the units. The units had to be assembled outdoors when the weather was favorable. A finished unit is pictured (below) in Roundtop Park, with the filtration plant in the background. Harold Thatcher, an educational advisor, had designed an individualized education program adapted to the interests and needs of each young man, both for their training for service on the job and their welfare at the termination of their enrollment. Enrollees were chosen for this project who had shown a desire to learn woodwork, with the hope that the acquired skills would open future job opportunities.

The supervisory personnel at CCC Camp SP4 were, from left to right (first row) junior foreman J.A. Eicker, landscape gardener Axel Christensen, junior foreman L.G. Temple, Supt. Mosher Edwards, facilitating mechanic Alex McGinnis, and junior foreman Jack Wallace; (second row) landscape engineer A.G. Stephens, engineer George Livingston, and facilitating carpenter Charles Patch. Salary rates were $2,300 a year for Superintendent Edwards; $2,000 a year for technical foremen; $1,860 for landscape gardener; and $1,680 for junior foremen. The facilitating personnel made $120 a month, and temporary skilled labor was paid hourly; the carpenter earned $1 an hour and the electrician earned $1.75 an hour.

On March 3, 1936, visitors to Camp SP4 are, from left to right, (first row) chief procurement clerk Robert Jensen, secretary of state planning board Dan Greenburg, Gov. Leslie Miller, sixth regional officer Donald Alexander, and Mayor Archie Allison; (second row) park authority for SP4 Aubrey Hildreth, educational advisor Harold Thatcher, second-in-command Lieutenant Reeder, and camp surgeon Major McCaskill; (third row) city engineer Z.E. Sevison, Wyoming State engineer Edwin W. Burritt, SP-ECW inspector Halsey M. Davidson, Supt. Mosher Edwards, and secretary of the Cheyenne Chamber of Commerce R.D. Hanesworth.

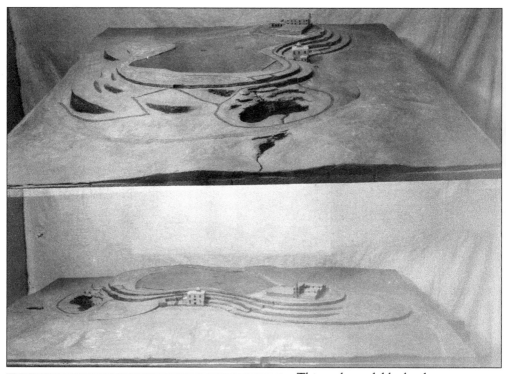

This scale model by landscape architect Andrew Larson shows the plans for the work to be done by CCC Camp SP4. Roundtop Hill would be terraced, sodded, and planted with trees. Foot trails, campgrounds, and picnic areas would be added around Roundtop Reservoir. Camp SP4 worked on these plans from August 1935 until the camp was removed in September 1937. Now called Camp Carefree, it is used by local Girl Scouts.

This photograph by Major Guthrie, a CCC officer from Washington, DC, shows the stone retaining walls below the Roundtop Filtration Plant as they neared completion. The stones for these walls came from the quarry at Granite Canyon and are visible from Roundtop Road. After the terraces were finished, trees were planted, and the ground was seeded with native grasses.

# Five
# WEATHER ON THE HIGH PLAINS

Frank Carruth (left) and Wayne Guernsey (right) are pictured in front of the office on September 2, 1940. A rock garden had been installed around the flagpole by CCC Camp NA2W with rocks collected from the Vedauwoo formation west of Cheyenne. The flag and trees show that this was taken on a windy day. The frequent, desiccating wind on the high plains is one of the largest factors that makes it difficult for plants to survive in this region.

In September 1942, the temperature dropped to negative 16 degrees Fahrenheit and hit negative 18 degrees a week later. This photograph was taken the following summer to show the winter kill of several Chinese elms along the road. Winter injury occurs when rapid frosts follow periods of warm weather. Sometimes only the top of the tree or certain branches are killed back, while the rest remains healthy and leafs out the following spring. Proper irrigation through the fall and winter helps prevent winter kill.

A micro Tessar 72-millimeter lens was used to photograph five chrysanthemum buds showing varying degrees of light to severe frost injury. The injured portions of the buds turn black. Since chrysanthemums flower late in the summer and Cheyenne frequently experiences early fall frosts, decades of research went into developing a series of mums that flowered earlier and were hardy enough to survive the long, cold winters.

On June 24, 1931, heavy rain and hail dumped 2.48 inches of precipitation in the span of two hours. Flooding along the main drive after the storm is pictured above. Hail is visible in the light patches on the grass in the foreground and at center. Cheyenne ranks first in the nation for frequency of hailstorms, averaging 9 or 10 storms each growing season. The office is on the right, and the tops of the headhouse and greenhouses are visible in the center background. Below, the flooded area behind the office is pictured, with the clerk's house on the right. The floodwater came down the hillside into the small valley behind the buildings.

After a storm on April 24, 1929, the drifts in front of the mess hall (above) extend to the top of the hill behind the buildings, pictured behind the foreman's house (below). At this time, much of the station was still under construction, and the weather demonstrated why horticultural research in Cheyenne was necessary. Cold-hardy fruits and vegetables already existed from the northern regions of the country, but few of them survived on the high plains. For most of the winter months, the bare ground is exposed to high winds and variations in temperature, with very little moisture. When snow does fall, the wind causes drifts that deposit moisture in some areas, while leaving others dry. This combination of factors made it very difficult for homesteaders attempting to plant trees and grow crops on the high plains.

An unidentified man uses a tractor to plow the service road behind the staff houses on March 9, 1932, after a two-day snowstorm. Shelterbelt trees can be seen sticking out of the snow, and Roundtop is visible in the background. Howell mentions in the station log after a storm in February 1940, that once station roads were cleared, it made driving much safer but less interesting.

A three-day storm, from April 23–25, 1935, produced drifts that completely covered the entrances to the packing shed and root cellar. A dog looks on while a crew of men works to dig them out. The barn is in the background. When other areas of the country are seeing bulbs and spring flowers, Cheyenne is getting snowstorms. Historically, Cheyenne receives the most snowfall between mid-March and mid-April.

The weather station, pictured on May 6, 1931, included many instruments to record environmental conditions. The evaporation tank is at center in the foreground. The shelter on the left housed a thermometer to record temperature and a psychrometer, which recorded the humidity in the atmosphere. The rain gauge is in the center background, with an anemometer at right to measure wind speed. The mess hall (left) and foreman's house (right) are in the background.

Snow fences have been used all over the world for centuries to control where blowing snow accumulates. A fence or row of plants, called a living snow fence, will slow the wind as it passes through, so more snow is deposited on the downwind side. On the lawns west of the superintendent's house, a good example of the impact of snow fences is shown. The snowdrifts piled up around the hedges and left a clear path where the wind swept through a six-foot gap in the hedge.

# Six
# Battling the Wind with Shelterbelts and Grasses

On August 16, 1933, a view of the station shelterbelts from behind the buildings shows how much had been established since the first plantings in 1930. The shelterbelt was a top priority after buildings were constructed. Protection from the frequent high winds was essential for the health of plants and the comfort of people. Many of these trees still stand today and make a substantial difference in the microclimate of the station.

A general view of the nursery where shelterbelt seedlings were grown is shown at left. The pipes on the left side of the bed are an overhead sprinkler system used throughout the nursery. The beds in the background to the left and right are covered. Station staff experimented with various materials to protect young plants from frost. The pine, spruce, and juniper seedlings below are an example of thousands of seedlings that were grown in the station nursery. Landowners in Wyoming, Nebraska, Wyoming, and Colorado were given trees and shrubs to plant in their shelterbelts. Data from the success of these plantings were included in the research conducted by station staff. Plants were also shared with many government agencies in the area, including the veterans hospital, highway department, state capitol, City of Cheyenne, Fort Warren, US Forest Service, Wind River Indian Agency, Soil Conservation Service, Colorado State University, and the University of Wyoming.

Inside the root cellar, workers pack trees for shipment on April 4, 1933. Young trees from the shelterbelt nursery were brought in during the fall, stored in the cellar over the winter, and packaged and shipped to cooperators in the spring.

Much of the seed for shelterbelt trees and shrubs had to be collected by station employees from plants growing at the station and in the surrounding area. Once collected, seed was cleaned for storage. In the packing shed, various equipment was used to clean seeds.

John Kelso and another employee, identified only as H.E., built this seed threshing machine for use at the station. The hopper or feeder entrance is on the left, the cylinder in the middle separated the seed from the chaff, and the threshed seed and chaff came out on the right. Combination V-pulleys allowed for changing the speed of the cylinder. Pictures were taken to send to Washington, DC, on October 2, 1934.

A box of cleaned seed sits in front of the machinery inside the packing shed. Sometimes seeds had to be counted. According to the station log on March 22, 1939, a CCC boy counting seed for Bohn developed a temperament and indicated cordial dislike for seed counting on nice days. He said he would be glad to count seed on snowy, windy days. Another boy in the afternoon proved more versatile in abilities and less so in temperament.

Many aspects of shelterbelt plantings were studied, including plant spacing, types of trees, and windbreak design. This photograph was taken to show the variation in root growth among different species of evergreen trees after one year. From left to right, plant No. 3 is yellow pine, No. 2 is blue spruce, and No. 1 is western red cedar.

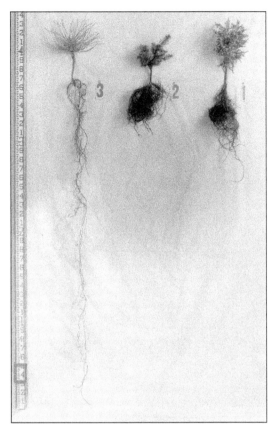

This windbreak is planted in the shape of an X. The design found most useful is an L shape, with rows to the north and west side of the land to be sheltered. Strong winds in this area usually come from the west or north. Shelterbelts provide multiple benefits: they reduce wind speed to prevent desiccation of plants from high winds, and they create a living snow fence, which produces snowdrifts around the plants, increasing moisture in the soil and insulating plant roots from rapid temperature fluctuations.

According to Shane Smith, Gene Howard developed a catchy way to identify evergreen trees by their needles. "P" is for pine, and "P" is for pockets. One could also say "P" is for poke, as pine needles are poky. The mugo pine (left) has bundles of two needles set into each pocket. The concolor fir (below) shows that "F" is for fir, and "F" is for flat and flexible. One could also say friendly because fir needles do not hurt the hand when touched. Fir needles are difficult to roll between the fingers because they are flat. An example of a spruce is not pictured, but he also said "S" is for spruce, and "S" is for square, stiff, and sharp. Spruce needles roll easily between the fingers due to their square shape, and their stiff needles have sharp tips that stab the fingers when touched.

The shelterbelt research included work with cooperators all over the region. Landowners were given trees and instructions on how to care for them. Station staff visited regularly to collect data on the progress of the shelterbelts. This is the property of Ernest Heiber near Burns, Wyoming. The shelterbelt was planted in 1929.

This photograph of the Theodore Smith farm northeast of Chappell, Nebraska, was taken in July 1943. The recommendation at the time was to till the ground around the trees to prevent weeds and grasses from competing with the trees for soil moisture. This was a common practice in dryland agriculture. Mulching is now recommended rather than tilling, to keep the soil moist, preserve its structure, and prevent soil erosion from wind or heavy rain.

W.G. Taylor of Bear Creek, Wyoming, poses with his daughter and dog in front of their windbreak in July 1933. At the higher altitudes on the high plains, the lower atmospheric pressure coupled with wind movement allows moisture to evaporate quickly from the soil, contributing to drought stress. The combination of wind, cold, and low humidity will desiccate and kill plants that are not adapted to such environments. A shelterbelt of hardy, drought-tolerant plants will lower the wind speeds and help more vulnerable plants survive the winters.

C. Loetscher of Burns, Wyoming, stands in front of a row of shrubs in his shelterbelt that was planted in 1920. The date of the photograph is August 9, 1933. These shrubs are probably *Caragana arborescens*, or Siberian pea shrub, which was a very popular choice for shelterbelts at the time. It was brought to the United States from Russia by Prof. Niels Hansen. He said it was grown extensively in Russia as a hedge plant, able to tolerate extreme drought, and very hardy.

On August 11, 1933, Reuben Anderson and his children stand in their shelterbelt, which was planted in 1926 near Pine Bluffs, Wyoming. Fast-growing shrubs were planted on the outermost row of the shelterbelt to create a natural snow fence and windbreak for the slower-growing evergreen trees on the inside.

Engstrom and Cris Jassmann pose in their newly planted shelterbelt near Lusk, Wyoming, in July 1933. To provide an effective windbreak, shelterbelt trees are planted closer together than usually recommended. Any plants that do not survive the first winter must be replaced within one or two years, or the larger plants around them will outcompete the replacements for sunlight and water.

Lee Fowler and his son stand in their shelterbelt near Douglas, Wyoming, in July 1933. This very large shelterbelt has eight rows of trees and shrubs. The current recommendation is to have a minimum of three rows to provide an effective windbreak.

Outside of Douglas, Wyoming, H.A. Hanlin stands in his young shelterbelt. The photograph was taken in July 1933. This shelterbelt is only a few years old, and the faster growth rate of the shrubs on the outside rows versus the trees on the inside rows is obvious.

John Soske's place was near Ardmore, South Dakota, in July 1933. The other man in the picture is unidentified. These men are standing in front of *Caragana*, or pea shrubs. There were four species recommended by the station in a list of horticultural plants dated 1972: *C. arborescens*, *C. frutex globosa*, *C. microphylla*, and *C. pygmaea*. *Microphylla* was collected in France by plant explorer W.T. Swingle. The rest were collected in Russia by Niels Hansen. Several species of *Caragana* are still available and recommended for homeowners today.

W.A. Shark's property was near Van Tassell, Wyoming, a tiny town on the Nebraska border near Lusk, and is pictured in July 1933. Evergreen trees are preferred for shelterbelts since they keep their foliage year-round and provide more wind protection in the winter. Deciduous shrubs can be used, as their branches grow close together and continue to block the wind in the winter, but deciduous trees are not recommended, since they lose their leaves over the winter, leaving space between the branches for the wind to sneak through.

On August 16, 1933, this general view of the cultivated fields was taken from Roundtop, looking south. At the time, station research included vegetables, fruits, ornamentals, and shelterbelts. A few years later, some of this land was used for research on grasses for erosion control and livestock forage.

This photograph of the irrigated grass plots for erosion studies was published in the October 1935 issue of *Soil Conservation* for an article on the Soil Conservation Service's efforts to establish erosion-control nurseries around the country. By the 1930s, human activities like poor farming practices, overgrazing, and construction projects were causing silting in rivers and reservoirs. The Soil Conservation Service and the Bureau of Plant Industry funded research and efforts to replant grasses and trees in steep areas where unprotected soils were likely to wash out.

*Echinochloa crusgalli*, commonly called barnyard grass, was native to Asia and studied as a possible grass for preventing soil erosion. It is now a widespread weed in crops all over the world. It absorbs a high amount of nitrogen from the soil, robbing the essential nutrient from neighboring plants and reducing crop yield.

An unidentified man stands next to sand grass in the irrigated forage crop plots. The forage grasses were studied by H.M. Benedict and were of great interest at the time. Researchers from all over the world visited the station to speak with Benedict about his research. The station log from September 10, 1937, mentioned a group of researchers visiting the station to view the plots. Members of the group were from Tucson, Arizona; Fort Collins, Colorado; Santa Barbara, California; and Johannesburg, South Africa.

The introduction of alfalfa from Turkestan by Niels Hansen changed American agriculture and was considered Hansen's most valuable discovery. The yellow-flowered Turkestan alfalfa was much more cold and drought-tolerant than European alfalfa, which made it possible to grow this valuable forage crop on the high plains. This photograph was of a particularly heavy alfalfa crop grown at the station in 1937.

Although the USDA plant explorers brought many foreign plants to the country that changed American agriculture for the better, the introduction of invasive species was also inevitable. *Swainsonia salsula,* or Swainson pea, is native to Asia and has become invasive in the western United States. Its seed is similar to alfalfa seeds, so it often becomes a seed contaminant in alfalfa fields.

*Bouteloua gracilis*, or blue gramma grass, is a native of the region that was studied in the grass trials. One study looked at the effects of nitrogen fertilizer. This photograph compares blue gramma grass treated with nitrogen (left) to untreated (right).

The plots on the left are introduced grasses, and those on the right are native grasses in dryland plots. Not surprisingly, the native grasses did better without irrigation than the introduced grasses did. The buildings in the background are the CCC camp, pictured on September 14, 1937.

Jackrabbits were plentiful on the plains and caused extensive damage to young trees. A rabbit has chewed the bark off around the trunk and lower branches of this apple tree, which is called girdling and is lethal to the tree. In the station log on March 23, 1938, Charles Adams was digging fruit trees to send to cooperators but only acquired 12 of the 150 desired; the rest had been killed by rabbits. Dr. Hildreth considered the research on rabbit repellent one of their most important projects at the time.

A fenced pen surrounded rows of young trees, and each row was treated with a different rabbit repellent. Station staff and members of the CCC conducted regular rabbit round-ups to capture jackrabbits and place them in the pen. At one drive mentioned in the station log on December 14, 1936, a total of 160 CCC men moved across two sections of pasture, catching 46 rabbits. About the same number managed to escape. This view of the rabbit pen shows which trees are still surviving.

# Seven
# GROWING YEAR-ROUND IN THE GREENHOUSE

The headhouse building with two greenhouses behind it was constructed in the fall and winter of 1930–1931. The headhouse contains a workspace, storage, an office, and a break room, which allowed employees to work outside of the warm, humid climate of the greenhouses and to maximize growing space inside them. The greenhouses run east to west to take advantage of southern exposure and capture as much sunlight as possible.

On October 22, 1930, framing of the greenhouses was underway as the headhouse neared completion. The large chimney was the exhaust for the coal-powered boilers that heated the greenhouses in the winter.

By December 10, 1930, the greenhouses are almost complete and are pictured from the southeast. Visible on the south side of the northern greenhouse is a row of cold frames. Heating pipes from the greenhouses ran through these cold frames so that the temperature could be controlled. The metal framing above the roofs of the greenhouses held a wire mesh to prevent hail damage to the glass.

This man, pictured on December 10, 1931, is digging a pit for soil temperature recording. He is standing about 50 feet west of the headhouse. The wires ran from the pit, through a conduit, into the headhouse where the potentiometer recorder was located.

The lath house was constructed in 1937 by CCC Camp NA2W. It has steel framework that was purchased through the Metropolitan Greenhouse Company for $1,958 and paid for with CCC funds. The lath slats are spaced to block out half of the sunlight and half of the wind, giving tender plants a place to acclimatize before being transplanted outside. The cypress slats have a concave groove running lengthwise on the top side so that snow and rain run off instead of pooling on the wood. This photograph was taken on September 28, 1940.

The two greenhouses were divided by a central corridor into four separate sections, originally referred to by their location of northwest, northeast, southwest, and southeast. Later, the four greenhouses were renamed A, B, C, and D, respectively. On January 4, 1933, cucumbers and watermelons are growing inside of Greenhouse D. This photograph was taken from the west end, looking east. The small box on the wooden platform on the right contained instruments that recorded the temperature and humidity over time on a roll of paper.

On February 2, 1933, the cucumbers and watermelons are shown after a month of growth. The vines climbed up the vertical strings, which greatly increased the number of plants that could be grown in a space and kept fruit off the soil surface. The pipes around the walls of the greenhouse carried hot water, which created radiant heat to warm the greenhouse in the winter months.

Taken on January 14, 1943, this picture shows a general view of peas planted in crocks in Greenhouse A as part of the pea filling experiment by Myron Babb. The soil was treated with formaldehyde as a source of nitrogen fertilizer, and the seeds were planted on January 1.

This side view of the crocks in the pea filling experiment also shows some of the features of Greenhouse A. Raised benches were constructed of wood. The gears visible on the windows in the right and rear of the photograph were part of the mechanism that opened greenhouse windows to release heat on warm days.

On July 8, 1942, the setup for a pea filling experiment is pictured above, showing the tubes and large jars used for irrigating and draining the pots. This experiment tested the effects of phosphorus fertilization on peas. The results of the experiment are pictured below on August 18, 1942. The six pots are typical representatives of the six treatments with various nutrient solutions. "N," "P," and "K" stand for nitrogen, phosphorus, and potassium, respectively, and are important nutrients for plant growth. Treatment 1 (left) contained all three nutrients, and treatment 2 (right) contained only nitrogen and potassium. Treatments 6, 5, 3, and 4 (center) were given phosphorus only at certain phases of development. The plants benefited most when all three nutrients were given throughout the testing period.

The squash and pumpkins harvested from Myron Babb's experiments are pictured in Greenhouse B. The station log mentions Jerry Brown spending six weeks in the fall measuring the sugar content of the pumpkins from Powers's pumpkin trials.

Seeding equipment used in the greenhouse is pictured on April 21, 1939, including flats, dibble boards, stroker, packer, and seeder. The dibble board had been used to create evenly spaced holes in the soil of the flat on the right.

The operation of spotting, or transplanting, tomato seedlings is demonstrated here. The plants are set in the holes created by the dibble board. The plants on the left have already been set in.

Seeding operation is demonstrated here. The flat is filled with soil, and the stroker is used to create rows. The row on the far left is seeded and covered. The next row is seeded but uncovered. The scoop-shaped seeder and packet of seeds are sitting in front of the flat.

# Eight
# VEGETABLES, FLOWERS, AND SMALL FRUITS

Two unidentified men remove discarded chrysanthemums from the field in October 1941. The chrysanthemum program started in 1932 and continued through 1970. In the 1960s, thousands of people would turn out each year during the open house to see over two acres of mums in full bloom. Not everyone appreciated them though. In 1935, Hastings brought in a bunch of chrysanthemum cuttings to sort in the office, and Howell complained about the unattractive aroma filling the building in the station log.

Pictured on December 10, 1931, a homemade soil and manure shredder is in action. Made from a cylinder and concaves of an old threshing machine, three men could not overfeed the rig as it pulverized clods of manure and sod to a consistency that could be used as a soil additive. Two men (above) feed the shredder on the left. The pile of shredded manure on the right has a much finer consistency, spreads more easily, and breaks down sooner in the soil. The pulverized fertilizer is loaded into a manure spreader (below) pulled by a team of horses for spreading over the fields. The greenhouse is visible in the left background, and Roundtop is in the center background.

An unidentified man spreads manure on the grounds along the main road in front of station buildings to prepare for planting. Spreading manure on the station grounds and test plots was a major winter job that took station laborers and CCC enrollees weeks to complete.

Another homemade piece of equipment is at work behind the Fordson tractor on April 8, 1932. This is a five-row tree marker. The marker is run in both directions across the field, and trees are planted at the intersections. Fordson tractors were built by Ford and were popular in the early 1900s due to their affordability. Vaughn and Witte were out on the tractors from dawn until dusk in March as soon as the ground thawed, plowing the fields for spring planting.

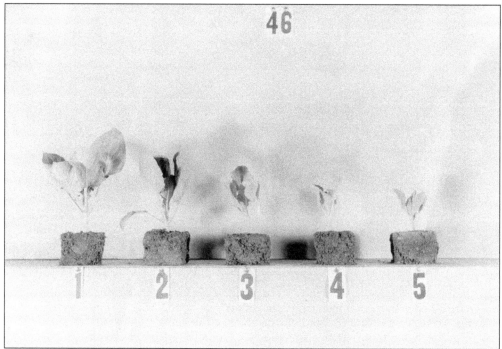

On June 26, 1933, specimens from each flat of Jersey Wakefield cabbage are pictured, showing the effects of five different treatments. They were treated with carbon, nitrogen, phosphorus, potassium, and hydrogen, respectively. They found that crops from the cabbage family produced best when started indoors and provided consistent water, temperature, and nutrients until planted outdoors to maximize yields and timely maturity. The variety of cabbage most recommended by M.F. Babb for Wyoming was Golden Acre.

One of the earliest experiments conducted by Babb was called the "hardening off" experiment. The plants were seeded in April in the greenhouse. Some were given fertilizer and sufficient moisture until being transplanted outside, and others were "hardened off" by gradually reducing moisture, fertilizer, and temperature before transplanting. They found that withholding moisture and nutrients delayed maturity and reduced yields. Late Snowball cauliflower is pictured in the field on September 18, 1931. Some of the plants are tied to bleach the heads.

Babb, Kraus, and Powers worked to develop varieties of tomatoes that could ripen within Cheyenne's short and cool growing season. The station log even mentions Babb sending tomato varieties to a researcher for the Campbell Soup Company. These tomatoes have been staked and pruned to one stalk in the field. Three varieties they bred and released were Alpine, Colorado Red, and Highlander.

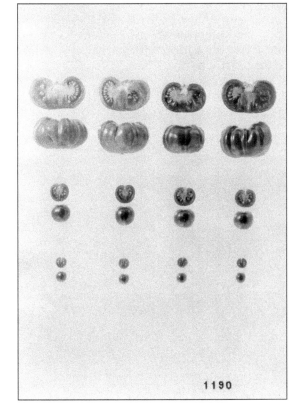

The fruits of tomato varieties Johannesfeuer (top), Red Currant (bottom), and the cross between them (center) are shown in a cross section on February 17, 1938.

A view of Babb's beans shows the vastness of the vegetable trial plots. Staff houses (left) and Roundtop (right) are visible far in the background. In 1930, Hildreth visited a 90-year-old Navajo woman at her farm on the Whiterocks Reservation. Rose Daniels was well known for her gardening skills. With her permission, Hildreth took seeds from three types of beans she had grown and stored. From those three varieties, he developed the first lima bean that can grow successfully on the high plains.

An unidentified dog lies in the shade of a row of corn while photographs of the vegetable garden are taken. M.F. Babb, together with W.L. Quayle, director of the Agricultural Experiment Station at the University of Wyoming, published a bulletin titled *Vegetable Culture and Varieties for Wyoming* in April 1942 based on research done at both locations. Many of the varieties they recommended are available through heirloom seed companies.

On January 20, 1942, rhubarb for one of Babb's experiments is in the new root cellar for forcing. Rhubarb is a perennial vegetable that can be grown with little irrigation because it is harvested in early spring when natural soil moisture is most plentiful. Irrigation during dry spells aids growth and increases yields the following spring.

Station staff experimented with various ways to protect tender plants from early- and late-season frost. These covers created a temporary cold frame to protect breeding melons from frost in the late summer. The covers must be lifted on warm sunny days to prevent the plants from becoming too hot and are closed overnight to trap warmth.

Examples of beets grown at the station are shown with root, cross section, and leaf. The varieties are, clockwise from bottom right, Black Knight, Black Red Ball, Argrow Wonder, and Detroit Red. In the 1942 vegetable publication, Babb recommended Crosby's Egyptian, Detroit Dark Red, Perfected Detroit, and Half-Long Blood Improved as the best varieties for Wyoming.

Witloof chicory, also called Belgian endive, was studied for its agricultural value. The taproots make a cheap substitute for coffee, and the top produces fresh salad greens. It was a high-priced crop that grew well in this region, valuing $600–$1,000 an acre in the 1930s, when over a million dollars' worth was imported annually from Europe. Despite the positive findings of this research, it did not take off among producers at the time, possibly because the biennial crop required more of a time investment than traditional annual vegetables.

On August 15, 1944, Max Hoover hand pollinates a bush-type squash plant. One of the earlier releases from the station was the Early Cheyenne pumpkin, bred by Dr. Powers. It was the first pie pumpkin that matured early enough to be grown successfully in Cheyenne and was released in 1939. Its smaller fruit was enough for one pie, perfect for home use. The plant itself is also smaller, which means it takes up less space in the garden. It was more productive and disease resistant than comparable varieties.

This photograph shows DeForest Alderman emasculating flowers on July 26, 1933. Flowers were dissected and hand-pollinated to cross specific varieties for breeding purposes. Covering the flowers with bags or tents (shown) prevented pollination by insects. This method is time-consuming and labor-intensive, but it saves years in the breeding program overall by increasing the rate at which desirable traits can be bred into the strain compared to natural cross-pollination. Pollinating crews had to start at 4:00 a.m. to complete the work before flowers wilted in the heat of the day.

Rows of the Cheyenne Hardy chrysanthemum series are pictured at the Kroh Brothers nursery in Loveland, Colorado. The station log mentions Kroh visiting with Hildreth frequently at the station, and they often exchanged plant material. The Cheyenne mums took decades to develop. Starting in 1932, Hildreth collected and tested 2,000 different varieties from all over the world. He allowed natural selection to determine which plants continued in the breeding program. Each season, the plants that survived the winter and flowered early enough to produce seeds were kept and allowed to cross-pollinate. He released the first varieties that were suited to Cheyenne's climate in 1947. Gene Howard then supervised the next step, improving the blossoms. The plants were crossed with varieties with showier flowers by hand-pollination to speed up the breeding process. After a few more years of breeding, over 20 varieties of the Cheyenne mum series were released to the public. These mums were featured at the Denver Botanic Gardens after Hildreth became the director. Both Howard and Hildreth took great personal pride in the Cheyenne mums.

The columbine is a native perennial to the Rocky Mountains. It is hardy and self-seeds, preferring partially shaded areas. The blue columbine is Colorado's state flower. The scientific name of columbine is *Aquilegia*, taken from the Latin word for eagle, due to the spurs on the back of the flower, which resemble an eagle's talons.

*Penstemon unilateralis* is so named because the flowers only grow on one side of the stem. Many different species of *Penstemon* grow as wildflowers in the western United States.

Four perennial flowers grown at the station are pictured. The first one is *Glandularia wrightii*, a native verbena with purple flowers. Second is *Linaria vulgaris*, yellow toadflax, which has escaped cultivation and often shows up on disturbed soils, causing some to consider it a weed. Third and fourth are *Ratibida columnifera* and *Ratibida pulcherrima*, respectively, and are commonly known as prairie coneflower or Mexican hat, which are native to the high plains with dark red flowers that bloom throughout the summer.

The flower in the top left (No. 2) is from the Apache plume plant, a native shrub pictured in the arboretum on page 123. The flowers on the bottom left and right of the photograph are *Mentzelia*, a bright yellow native flower commonly called blazing star.

Raspberries were difficult to grow in areas with harsh winters because the fruit was often produced on stems from the previous season. When winter kill took out canes from the previous year, it reduced the amount of fruit produced by the plant. The raspberry covering machine is in operation on November 14, 1933. The plants in front of the machine are being covered with soil to protect them from frost damage over the winter.

Raspberry research began with Hildreth and Powers, and nearly 10 acres of land were filled with raspberry plants. Hardy raspberries were eventually developed and made available to commercial nurseries, including the Trailblazer and Pathfinder (pictured) varieties. These plants flower and produce fruit on first-year wood, so that winter kill does not inhibit production. The last variety released by Gene Howard was Plainsman in 1993.

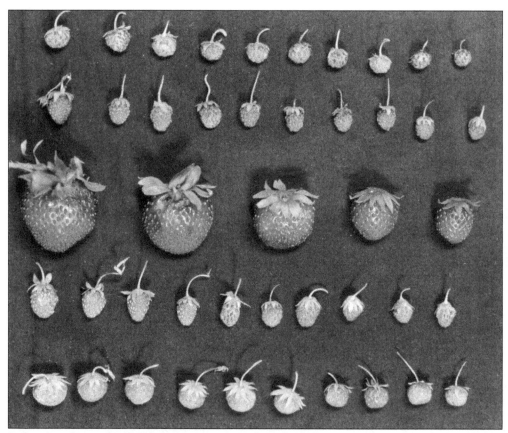

Before the advent of refrigerated shipping, the only fresh produce many residents had access to was what they could grow themselves. Hildreth and Powers collected over 42,000 native strawberry plants from Montana to New Mexico and crossed them with commercial varieties to develop strawberries that could grow and produce well in Cheyenne. The types of native strawberry fruits are compared to commercial strawberries in this picture from June 29, 1940. The types, from top to bottom, are flat, triangular, a commercial variety, long round, and round.

The results of these breeding efforts were the Fort Laramie (pictured) and Ogallala strawberries. They both are everbearing so that the home gardener can grow quality strawberries throughout the season. Fort Laramie was released in 1973 by Gene Howard. It was extremely winter hardy with large, bright red fruit. The plant also recovers well from hail damage.

# *Nine*
# THE ARBORETUM, A LIVING LEGACY

Andy Krofcheck stands next to a specimen of *Prunus padus*, commonly called Mayday tree or bird cherry, which was collected by Niels Hansen from Siberia in 1898. This specimen, pictured on July 1, 1942, had the desirable trait of not producing suckers. Ornamental trees and shrubs were tested in the arboretum to see if they could grow on the high plains. Although many of the plants that were there in 1974 had perished by 2000, those that remain are a living legacy of over 40 years of testing at the station.

Palemon Howard Dorsett was a USDA plant explorer who traveled all over the world, including Manchuria, China, which has very cold, dry winters. He is pictured above riding the donkey on the right, with his Chinese interpreter, Peter Liu, riding the donkey on the left, as they are guided down the trail near Pa Ta Chu, Western Hills, to the west of Peiping (now Beijing). His three-year expedition with William Joseph Morse collecting and learning about soybeans grown in Asia helped soybeans become an agricultural staple in America. At the Temple of Heaven in Peiping (below), the larger plant growing out of the moat wall on the left is the euonymus that Dorsett collected seeds from on November 1, 1924. The yellowish-green leaves with pink stems and bright red berries caught his attention. From these seeds, Howard and Vanderslice developed and released the "Pink Lady" winterberry euonymus in 1973. (Both, courtesy of Special Collections, USDA National Agricultural Library.)

These pagodas stand outside the Buddhist temple of Fa Hua Ssu, where P.H. Dorsett collected seeds from a crab apple with attractive fruits. A tree grown from Dorsett's seeds was planted at the station in 1933, and the Hung Hai Tung crab apple is the most spectacular crab apple in the arboretum, with two-inch-wide white blossoms every spring. The parent tree grew in a sacred place, and the specimen growing at the arboretum also evokes a feeling of reverence. (Courtesy of Special Collections, USDA National Agricultural Library.)

On Hansen's first trip to Russia, he found a crab apple growing in the Imperial Botanic Garden in St. Petersburg. From these seeds, the ornamental variety Dolgo was developed. On his second trip, he learned of a unique variety with red flesh, wood, new leaves, and flowers growing in Alma Alta, near the Tian Shan Mountains between Russia and China. The scientific name was *Malus niedzwetzkyana*, after the amateur naturalist Vladislav Niedzwetzky, who discovered it. Commonly called the red-veined crab apple, it became the source of all domestic crab apples with reddish-pink flowers.

An unidentified man stands between rows of poplar trees in the nursery on August 31, 1932. The species pictured here is unknown, but Niels Hansen collected seeds of the balsam poplar from Siberia in 1897. The station also tested many varieties of cottonwood trees, which are closely related to poplars. The Highland cottonwood, *Populus acuminata x sargentii*, was bred and released from the station.

Several specimens of *Elaeagnus angustifolia* still stand gracefully in the arboretum. Russian olive was collected by Niels Hansen in China and Russia in 1898 and became popular in the western part of the country, where it was successful in windbreaks and erosion control. Unfortunately, it easily seeds and invades riparian areas along bodies of water, spreading quickly and choking out native plants. The deep root system makes it difficult to eradicate, and it has been listed as a noxious weed in many states.

*Syringa oblata* "Cheyenne," commonly called the Cheyenne lilac, was released by the station in 1971 by Gene Howard. This plant was developed from seed collected by P.H. Dorsett and W.J. Morse on their expedition to northern China in 1930. They found the original lilac at the Southern Manchurian Railway Agricultural Experiment Station in Yugakujo, Manchuria. The leaves have an attractive purplish-red fall color. Hazel Pacheco is pictured with the Cheyenne lilac covered in flowers in June 1975.

Esther Martinez is pictured on May 18, 1979, with the prairie almond in full bloom. This plant is the result of a cross between *Prunus triloba* and *Prunus pedunculata*, the seeds of which came from the experimental farm station in Brandon, Manitoba, Canada. The seeds of this plant are poisonous, like most wild almonds.

Gene Vanderslice is pictured with *Juniperus scopulorum*, or Rocky Mountain juniper, near the Alcova Dam in central Wyoming. This juniper is native to western North America, from Canada to northern Mexico. Many varieties and cultivars of this plant are available, including Woodward, Wichita Blue, and Skyrocket. The Woodward juniper was developed at the station and is on the Plant Select list with the Cheyenne mock orange and Apache plume. Plant Select is a registered trademark brand of plants especially recommended for the high plains region.

Commonly called mock orange because of its citrus-scented flowers, *Philadelphus pekinensis* is native to China and Korea. The North American version of the mock orange is *Philadelphus lewisii*, named for American explorer Meriwether Lewis. The seeds for this species were obtained from Alberta, Canada. Gene Howard said there were 200 mock oranges tested in the arboretum. Many suffered irreparable damage due to deer browsing. "Cheyenne" was the most successful variety because the deer leave it alone, and it is very drought tolerant.

Marilyn Samuel stands next to *Fallugia paradoxa*, commonly known as Apache plume, in the early 1970s. It is native to the American Southwest and can be found in the deserts. Staff from the Cheyenne station probably collected the seeds or obtained them from researchers in New Mexico. It is a showy native shrub with pale pink to white blossoms from spring to fall and feathery, pink seed heads throughout the winter.

This patch of *Robinia neomexicana*, or New Mexico locust, is growing on Roundtop Hill. It is native to the American Southwest and can be found growing wild in Texas, California, and Colorado. Native Americans in the Southwest region ate the flowers and pods, and this plant is also eaten by livestock and wildlife. It grows well in this area and can spread long distances through underground runners, so it is best planted where it can be allowed to form a thicket.

Over 800 different varieties of apples were tested at the station, most grown on Siberian rootstock (left). Susan Allen quotes Gene Howard in the *Leaf-Let* as saying, "We harvested 105,000 pounds of apples in 1958. Now that's a lot of apples." Only a few of the trees from the original orchard remain (below). One of those came from an experimental farm in Indian Head, Saskatchewan, Canada. A neighboring orphanage cared for children whose parents had to travel to find work in the 1930s, and the children would pick and eat the fruit at the station. Researchers noticed that when the children got to a cross between a hardy crab apple and the Russian Repka Kis Laga apple, they would empty their pockets of apples from the other trees and fill them with fruit from that tree. They decided to name the variety "Renown" due to its renown among the children. (Below, courtesy of Janelle Rose Photography.)

The sign for the Cheyenne Horticultural Field Station lies in a junk pile (above) after the name was changed to the High Plains Grasslands Research Station in 1974. According to Susan Allen in the *Leaf-Let*, Gene Howard said, "Folks didn't need all the testing anymore. Why . . . with improved transportation from California, or wherever, you could get all kinds of fresh fruits and vegetables right at the grocery store. They didn't need the home garden anymore except for as a hobby." Howard was given orders to send cuttings of the best trees in the orchard and bulldoze it, but he decided to leave some of his favorite varieties standing. The cattle that came to the station for grazing research appreciated the shade (below), but the remaining trees in the orchard slowly died off until less than a handful remain today. The City of Cheyenne Urban Forestry Division replanted an apple orchard in 2015 using some of the original varieties.

One of the most noticeable aspects of the arboretum today is the rows of cottonwood trees (above) along the irrigation ditches. In some places, their arched trunks form a tunnel of shady foliage in the summer. The Encampment willow (below) was a native white willow found near Encampment, Wyoming. Despite minimal irrigation, it has grown to become one of the largest shade trees surviving in the arboretum. Sixty-two acres containing the original arboretum were returned to management by the City of Cheyenne in 2008, and efforts are ongoing to preserve the remaining trees. It is now known as the High Plains Arboretum and is open to the public. The physical address is 8301 Hildreth Road. All royalties and profits from this book will go to the maintenance of the arboretum. To make an additional contribution, please contact the Friends of the Cheyenne Botanic Gardens. (Both, courtesy of Cheyenne Urban Forestry.)

# BIBLIOGRAPHY

Agricultural Research Service US Department of Agriculture. *High Plains Grasslands Research Station Cheyenne, Wyoming.* June 18, 1988. www.ars.usda.gov

Allen, Susan. "Cheyenne's Horticultural Pioneers." *Leaf-Let Newsletter.* Cheyenne, WY: McIntyre's Garden Center. 1996.

Babb, M.F., and W.L. Quayle. "Vegetable Culture and Varieties for Wyoming." University of Wyoming Agriculture Experiment Station. Bulletin No. 250. Laramie, WY. April 1942.

Curtis, Ann. "Native Pioneers: Rose Daniels" *Daughters of Utah Pioneers.* (October 1983): 41–46

Freeman, John F. *High Plains Horticulture: A History.* Boulder, CO: University Press of Colorado, 2008.

Howard, Gene S., and G.B. Brown. "Twenty-eight Years of Testing Tree Fruit Varieties at the Cheyenne Horticultural Field Station, Cheyenne, Wyoming." *Crops Research.* Agricultural Research Service US Department of Agriculture. ARS 34–39. October 1962.

National Agricultural Library Special Collections. "Dorsett-Morse Oriental Agricultural Exploration Expedition Collection." US Department of Agriculture. specialcollections.nal.usda.gov. 2006.

Peterson, Barbara. "Cheyenne: The High Plains Arboretum." Wyoming in Motion Web Magazine. wyominginmotion.com

Powers, LeRoy. "Early Cheyenne Pie Pumpkin." US Department of Agriculture. Circular No. 537. Washington, DC: November 1939.

seagerwheelerfarm.org

Skogerboe, Scott. "Plant Explorers: Brave Revolutions and Uprisings." *The Colorado Gardener.* April 1998. Reprinted in the *GardenSMART* eNewsletter. www.gardensmart.com

sdexcellence.org/N.E._(Niels)_Hansen

Thompson, Lisa. "Public Works Administration." livingnewdeal.org. November 18, 2016.

US Department of Agriculture, Division of Botany. "Foreign Seeds and Plants Imported by the Section of Seed and Plant Introduction." Nos. 1–1,000. *Plant Inventory.* Issues 1–8. 1898.

*The Wyoming Eagle,* "Wyoming Listed as Definitely for Roosevelt after His Visit." Cheyenne, WY. Volume 13, No. 83. October 13, 1936.

Visit us at
arcadiapublishing.com

CPSIA information can be obtained
at www.ICGtesting.com
Printed in the USA
BVHW052022130522
636974BV00002B/50